Sea of Serenity

Seasons of Poetry Series

*Chad Joseph Thieman
& Tina Bryant*

Cover design & poetry by Chad Joseph Thieman
Layout & devotions by Tina Bryant
Cover photograph by Curtis Thieman
Copyright ©2017 All Rights Reserved
Thieman & Bryant

*** Special thanks to Debra Moore and Peggy Clark for helping in proofing and editing.

This series is dedicated to you, our readers. Tina and I are so thankful for the opportunity to share, encourage, and inspire. Your support of our personal ministry is greatly appreciated.

- *Chad*

Contents

Introduction:

"Sometimes we feel like we are going through our trials alone, that everything else in our lives doesn't really matter. Sometimes we can't see that far in the distance to know what is going to happen next. We may tend to worry too much, or not trust in God as much as we should.

Reflect on those times when you were going through rough storms in life. Did you ever wonder who would help guide you through them or how you were going to carry your burdens? When we focus on the one true answer, which is Christ, then we will start to understand the one who will guide us through these storms of life and into the Sea of Serenity. Join me as I take you on an inspirational and reflective journey through the poetic works of Chad Joseph Thieman, the Poet of Light."

- Tina Bryant

A Lighted Fortress

There is a lighted fortress

Standing in the midst of the sea,

Towering above restless waters,

Beaconing to you and to me.

Far across a great distance,

Its beacon is clearly seen.

Over dark and shadowy waters,

This priceless gem does gleam.

An answer to our prayers,

Through life's long and stormy nights;

Guiding vessels safely home,

Showing the way, by its light.

Deuteronomy 31:8

Think about a time when you went through a storm in life, and felt like no one was there to help you through it. What did you do? Did you try to take care of the situation on your own, or did you seek God's Spirit for guidance and ask Him to help navigate you through?

Write about what the situation was and how it turned out.

Journal

A Lonely Vessel

Like a lonely vessel, I sail all alone;
Across this vast ocean, to and fro I roam.
When there seem to be signs of life,
I send the lifeboats out;
Only to find nothing at all in the end,
Except for fear and doubt.
This ocean is but a graveyard,
Of those glorious ships of the past.
Whatever happened to those ships,
Whatever happened? I dare to ask.
I look forward to peace and tranquility,
Now that the storm has finally passed;
But it seems to be me, by myself,
With no other vessels left.
Still, I voyage out, across that peaceful calm,
With fervent expectation and hope;
That one day, I'll see on the distant horizon,
A line of sails from those grand ships arising!

Ecclesiastes 4:9-10

When we are facing storms in life, we need a circle of friends, those who can pray for us. Jesus once said, "For where two or three are gathered together in my name, I am there in the midst of them." When we have believers comforting us, we never feel alone.

Do you have people in your life, who are willing to join in Christ-centered fellowship with you? Who are they?

Journal

A Sea of Inspiration

A sea of inspiration floods through me every day,

With spiritual revelations and the Father's amazing grace.

I'm a willing and humble vessel with a hoisted up sail,

Catching the wind of every word, as wisdom doth prevail;

Against a world of turbulent waters,

Caused by many-a-passing storm.

This great sea of inspiration flows in diverse and infinite forms.

It gives wind to my sail, up to the peak of the boat,

Propelling me forward through uncharted unknowns;

As Your sea of inspiration always moves me to unveil,

The fullness of the Gospel, to those where darkness dwell.

Hebrews 10:24-25

When the light of Christ is shining through us, people take notice. We can lift their spirits by calling and telling them that we are thinking about them. We can share Scripture or pray with those we come in contact with. Maybe we can send them a letter in the mail. We never know the influence or impact that love can have when someone receives a random act of kindness!

What are some ways that you can be a sea of inspiration in someone else's life?

Journal

A Seashell or an Oyster

If you were offered a seashell or an oyster,

Of which of these two would you choose?

Most would choose the seashell of course,

For it is the prettier one of the two.

Whether it has a smooth or rough surface,

Its beauty will surpass most always, it's true!

An oyster, on the other hand, many would pass by,

Because it is the more loathsome of the two.

Though if it were me, I think I would pick the oyster,

In hopes that a pearl might be hidden inside;

But if it were you, which one would you choose,

Or how would you decide?

1 John 2:15-16

Being "worldly" is living for the world; living "Godly" is being Christ-like in our actions. We cannot be both. It is so easy to choose "worldly" pleasure because it is more appealing and we think that's what will make us happy. As believers, we know that Jesus will be returning soon, and the things of this world will pass away.

In which ways are you drawing closer to God and rejecting the ways of the world?

Journal

A Walk along Pelican Bay

Two little girls walk the shores of Pelican Bay,

Holding hands and talking, Serenity and her sister Grace;

Each in matching beachwear and closeness in age,

Serenity the eldest and Grace full of faith.

The two girls pick up seashells,

As they talk about their day;

Starting in a carefree stroll, before picking up the pace.

An inspiring conversation leads to a full-fledged race;

As they sprint toward a nearby beach house,

Where they spend most of their days.

These two adopted little girls,

Reach their destination and embrace.

They change into their evening dresses,

And from the porch swing, watch the waves;

As the sun begins to set, at the end of a perfect day.

Psalms 127:3-5

As adults, we sometimes get busy and forget to walk daily with the Lord because we often get wrapped up in our own struggles. Children typically are filled with innocence and wonder. They find it easier to look to Jesus daily.

Write down a basic plan to set aside more time for your Heavenly Father, and to become more childlike in His presence. If you have children of your own, how has their time of innocence been a blessing to you?

Journal

A Wasted Day

As I watch the sun's descent,
At the end of this wasted day;
Standing here in my solitude,
Beside the ocean, I pray.

"Father, what exactly do I do,
With such a wasted day;
This day I let go by,
In sluggish and sinful ways?

Forgive me for tossing aside,
Those hours of opportunity;
I could've been a positive force,
Working for the good humanity.

I may have impacted a little child,
Or perhaps a neighbor or friend;

And inspired them to do better,

By simply encouraging them.

I could have helped a stranger,

And offered some nourishment;

But my flesh got in the way,

And Lord, for this I do repent."

As I look across the rolling waves,

I feel the Lord begin to speak:

"My child, you didn't waste a day,

For there's no day, I can't redeem.

Your prayer will impact the world.

And one day your eyes will see;

How this was a part of my plan,

As you find your place in eternity."

Isaiah 44:22

God is so much bigger than us. Have you heard that before? The truth is that nothing is impossible for Him. Our Heavenly Father redeems. He can take what we see as a wasted day and turn it into something beautiful and amazing! We may not see the full outcome of what He does in the here and now, but we will once we enter the Kingdom of God. Never underestimate God in what He is capable of doing.

How has our Heavenly Father redeemed one of your days? Did you remember to thank Him?

Journal

An Ocean of Dreams

Two newlyweds dance along the evening sea.

The view beheld is a sight to be seen,

Like a musical entitled *An Ocean of Dreams.*

Both king in his robe and queen in her gown,

Move ever gracefully to the calming sound,

Of passing waves beneath heaven's gold crown.

The moonlit waters are glimmering behind,

Like a ballet of starlets in shimmering light,

An illuminating reflection of heavenly heights.

The bridegroom and his bride burst forth in song.

They sing of their love as they glide along,

Remaining in tune and continuing until dawn;

When at the conclusion of that magical scene,

They both bow before applauding palm trees,

A standing ovation for *An Ocean of Dreams.*

Psalms 98:4

Did you know that worshiping is an expression of love and service to God?

Singing praise is one of the greatest ways we can express relief and joy, both during a trial and after our troubles have passed.

What inspirational lyrics do you sing when you are praising God?

Journal

Anchor of my Soul

As I sail across these deep waters,

I will lift my eyes up toward you;

For my hope is placed in no other,

And your hand will guide me through.

When the sea becomes unpassable,

And great waves threaten to devour;

I will call to the anchor of my soul,

"Lord give me strength in this hour!

Keep this vessel afloat on the sea,

As darkened clouds come rolling in;

Anchor me firmly upon my knees,

And deliver thy servant from every sin.

Do not let fear overtake this soul,

Increase my faith throughout the storm;

And I will surrender with righteous hope,

As your love and mercy guide me home.

Proverbs 3:5-6

How many times have you had to make important decisions in your life that required coming to the Lord for Guidance?

We often want to do things on our own, without seeking help from the Creator. Remember that our Heavenly Father knows what is best for each of us.

Write about some difficult decisions that you had to make in the recent or distant past, through prayer and fasting.

Journal

Angels in the Sand

As she sits beneath the warmth of a midday sun,
On the edge of an endless sea;
She watches her two daughters at play,
And it stirs up childhood memories.

As these thoughts start coming to mind,
She's taken back to another place in time;
Laying face up in the sand,
With waving arms and outstretched hands.

It was her siblings and her at play,
Making sand angels down by the bay.
Moving their arms with a back and forth motion,
Until three angels appeared, down by the ocean.

By time they had finished, a clear outline remained,
Until that high tide, in the late evening came.
For her siblings and her, it was a fun game,
But looking back now so much has changed.

She musters a smile and comes back to today,
Watching her two precious angels at play.

Matthew 18:3

Jesus has called us to be childlike in order to inherit the Kingdom of Heaven. Children have innocence and can truly trust God in about everything they do. As adults, we tend to have a more difficult time trusting our Heavenly Father.

What are some of the ways that you can become more childlike for Christ? What are some of the greatest memories that you have, from when you were a young child?

Journal

Beside the Evening Sea

She walks the shoreline late at night,

And dreams her dreams beneath the moonlight;

Waiting patiently for her prince to arrive,

A sail to appear above the rolling tide.

Her gown is white against the black night,

Her feet are bare, and love is her only care;

As she walks the shoreline sipping a glass of red wine,

Her long hair blowing in the evening wind,

As she waits earnestly for him.

Soon he will be with her and embrace her passionately,

Beneath the starry sky, beside the evening sea.

Psalms 27:14

Have you had to wait on something that you felt needed to happen right away? What was the outcome? Was it worth the wait?

There are many reasons why God has us wait on our desires. We may not know the reason at the moment, but we need to trust in Him and ask for the gift of patience.

Journal

Beyond Serenity's Shore

From here to eternity flow the waters of Serenity,

Rolling on beneath me, as I sail this open sea.

There is so much more, many things yet to explore,

Beyond Serenity's shore.

The wind blows mightily, leading me further away;

I can no longer stay.

I will glide with open sail

And find my life, whether I succeed or fail.

Lord, I give it all to you.

There is nothing left for this man to do.

I'll ride these waves across the endless sea,

And discover there what it means to be free.

Jeremiah 29:11

God has a plan for each and every one of us. We all have a journey to take. We just need to get out of His way and allow Him to show us that narrow path, which He is calling us to take.

What plans are you trying to control in life? How can you turn them over to God and truly begin to track with His Spirit?

Journal

Come and Sail with Me

Come and sail with me
Across Serenity.
We'll head toward the horizon,
While the sun is yet arising.
Lord, come and sail with me.

Come and sail with me,
Nowhere else I'd rather be;
Then here alone with you,
Upon this open sea.
Lord, come and sail with me.

Come and sail with me
Across Serenity,
As your Spirit flows free
Throughout all eternity;
Lord, come and sail with me.

John 16:32

Jesus Christ tells us that he is never alone because the Father is with him. We sometimes forget that God is with us; we feel that we are going through rough times by ourselves. Even Jesus went through rough times. He knew God was with him every step of the way. When we think God is far away, we need to stop what we are doing and be still. We must be quiet and listen for His Spirit.

Write about a time when you really felt that God was near.

Journal

Faith Walks on Water

Faith walks on water,
Across the raging sea;
When I hear the Lord,
Calling out to me.
He's calling out my name,
Through the wind and rain;
Telling me to come,
Into his open arms.
Faith walks on water,
And fear has no place;
For he has raised me up,
Into the realm of grace.
Even through the storm,
As great darkness covers;
I see him standing there,
Calling me across the waters.

Matthew 14:26-33

Sometimes it is hard for us to know that Jesus is here calling to us. When we take our next step in our journey, we need to take it in faith. Jesus told his disciples to trust him and to have faith.

Do you have faith in the Lord? What does faith mean to you, and how has it changed and influenced your life?

Journal

His Footprints

The Messiah walked on water,
But Peter sunk with haste.
Come to Christ, he could not,
For he lacked greatly in faith.

The wind, it blew so strong,
And the waves, they were so vile;
Yet, Christ told him to come,
With the faith of a little child.

But Peter became terrified,
And sinking, he threw out his hand.
Christ shook his head and had mercy,
And reached down to rescue the man.

Sometime later Christ walked beside him,
As they walked down a stretch of beach.
He encouraged and gave him instruction,
"Peter, please feed my sheep."

And to make sure this time,
His disciple could follow God's plan.
The Messiah left His footprints,
Behind, in the sand.

Proverbs 3:5-6

Did you know that God has a purpose for your life? Have you asked Him what your purpose is, and how to use your talents and gifts to fulfill it?

In order for us to understand what God has called us to do, we first need to start following the footprints that Christ left behind and trust him.

Pray about God's purpose in your life, and write out a plan about how you can better fulfill it.

Journal

I am a Lighthouse

I am a lighthouse,
Standing faithful and true;
Set upon solid rock,
Shining my light upon you.

I am a lighthouse,
A beacon in the darkest night.
My keeper, He never sleeps,
And my lamp burns ever bright.

I am a lighthouse,
My signal will pierce the storm;
Shining forth a guiding light,
To vessels lost and torn.

I am a lighthouse,
My lamp set high above the sea.
A guardian am I over vessels,
Who wander aimlessly.

John 8:12

What do you believe it means that Jesus is the light of the world?

Just as a lighthouse will help us find our way, Jesus will do the same. He brings God's presence, protection, and guidance. He shows us how to be a lighthouse to others by truly loving and forgiving them, even our greatest enemies.

Is Jesus your lighthouse? In what ways can you be a lighthouse to others for the Lord?

Journal

Island of White

She's an island of white,

Shining ever so bright;

A beacon of light,

Through the darkest of nights.

I am the castaway,

Upon her white sands;

A welcomed guest,

To this once foreign land.

Standing faithful and true,

Amidst a sea of deep blue;

She's an island of white,

In the brilliance of light.

This island of white,

She continues to shine;

Through the darkest of nights,

A great treasure to find.

Psalms 23:4

Have you ever been some place that had no lights? Did you feel a little scared?

God has promised us that He will always be there to protect and comfort us. He is our light in the darkness.

Do you feel that God is with you during your dark times? Why or why not?

Journal

Living in a Daydream

Another day busy as a bee;
Another day where I don't care to be.
Another moment lost in daydream;
Another day living in a memory.

...I'm barefoot in the sand,
Lying beside my best friend.
It's a smoldering summer day.
I feel the stress melt away.

Sunlight bathes my skin,
As the water greets my feet.
It's another day in paradise,
With the one, I love, next to me.

Voices of laughter on the wind,
Children playing in the sand;
The waves and seagulls calm me,
As I envision this day by the sea...

Another day resting on the beach;
Another day isn't out of my reach.
Another moment of fun in the sun;
Another day of work is done!

Psalms 46:10

Finding peace can be hard during a busy work day. We tend to get through some of our days by daydreaming. God wants us to find time to be still. We need to take time out of our busy days for prayer, even if it is only for a few minutes a day. Our Heavenly Father may have something important to share with us.

What are some ways that you can find time for God, in the midst of your busiest days?

Journal

My Sandcastle Princess

Building a sandcastle, she looks up with a smile;

"Daddy, can you come and play for a while?"

I told her I would, and to put her feet on mine;

And I danced in the sand with that princess of mine.

My sandcastle princess, how the time has flown by;

Her wedding day is here and she's starting to cry.

I wipe away her tears, not knowing what to say.

My sandcastle princess is getting married today.

The years have passed by, and seasons have changed;

But time has a way of healing the pain.

Building a sandcastle, she looks up with a smile;

"Grandpa, can you come and play for a while?"

I told her I would, and to put her feet on mine;

And I danced in the sand with that princess of mine.

1 John 3:1

Some may have a dad on this earth who is always there for them. He may guide them, pray for them, and protect them. Others may not have one, but we all can have a Heavenly Father, who guides, protects, and loves us. God calls us to be His children.

Make a list of some of the good things that your earthly dad and Heavenly Father have done for you, and how those things made you feel at the time.

Journal

Ode to the Lighthouse

There's a lamp in a tower,

Out on the bay.

Like a star over the waters,

It shines like the day.

Helping lost sailors,

To find their way.

It's leading them home,

Putting an end,

To their tireless roam.

It's guiding them safely,

Through the storm-filled night;

A beacon over the harbor

Shining pure light.

John 1:5

There is spiritual light and there is spiritual darkness. The light is Jesus Christ, who shines his light on the right path. The darkness is Satan, who will guide us down the path of sin. Jesus Christ our Lord removes darkness (sin) so that we can follow him down the path of eternal life.

In what ways have you allowed Jesus or one of his followers to shine the light of Christ into your life?

Journal

Sandcastles

Seeking success, I devise my own plan,
Building a castle on a foundation of sand.
I am a creator, I say in my heart,
Then a wave comes and tears my castle apart.

Each time I tell myself, this time it will last;
For many castles have fallen in the past.
Yet still, each night that tide rolls in,
And I have to begin building all over again.

My pride has blinded me from the truth,
I think there's something that I need to prove.
So I build a sandcastle again with my hands,
And admire the masterpiece created by man.

Every night the tide comes and washes it away,
And I start all over again, on the very next day.
Ignoring humility and God's loving plan,
I keep building sandcastles, here in the sand.

Luke 6:49

A foundation is a base on which some structure sits. A building cannot stand well without a firm foundation. In the faith, obeying God is like building a house on a strong, solid foundation that stands firm when the storms come. Life can be calm at times, but during the storms, our foundations are tested. By knowing and trusting Jesus, our faith will stand strong.

What are some of the things that you can to do, to make sure you have a strong and solid foundation in the faith?

Journal

Sandpiper

There is a mostly forgotten myth,
Which survived barely to this day;
About a young master and his bird,
Made of water, sand, and clay.

"Sandpiper, oh sandpiper,
Won't you come alive and play?"
The young master called out,
In the midst of a calming seascape.

Other children laughed with disbelief,
At the sight of the boy and his bird;
But the young master ignored them,
As he again repeated those words:

"Sandpiper, oh sandpiper,
Won't you come alive and play?"
The young master proclaimed,
As he ascended higher in faith.

In a moment everything changed,
By the vibration of what was said;
In that instant, the bird came alive,
Scurrying along the water's edge.

Acts 5:40-42

The disciples were warned a number of times not to talk about Jesus, but they boldly continued to tell the world about all that the Lord had done. Jesus Christ commands us to share the Gospel by telling the world about him, the Father, and their shared Holy Spirit.

Are you ready and willing to help spread the "Good News," and be persecuted for your faith in the Lord? In what ways have you already been persecuted for the faith?

Journal

Sea of Grace

He is the anchor of every vessel,
Battered and worn by the waves.
He is the glow of every lighthouse,
Shining brightly, showing the way.
He is the glory of the sunrise,
Heralding in each new day;
And the wind across the waters,
Guiding sails along the way.
He is the joy of every dolphin,
Jumping high and giving praise.
He is the moon pull on the tide,
Telling the waters where to lay.
He is the fullness of the sea,
And we are mere drops you see;
Like wandering vessels,
Weathering storms faithfully.
His wrath is like a hurricane,
His mercy like the calm of its eye;
Filled with the brightness of the sun,
Against the clear blue sky.
He is the hope of every sailor,
Above life's dark and murky waters.
He is the answer to their prayers,
Helping them not to falter.
He is the ocean of Spirit,
And His character, we can't come near it;
Unless we receive Him with faith,
And embrace His Sea of Grace.

Hebrews 4:16

*God wants to be close to us. He is our protector.
We might not always feel his presence, but He is
there with us. When we start to feel overwhelmed,
we need to seek His Spirit.*

*Do you find it hard to talk to God? Write about a
time that you needed grace and talked to your
Heavenly Father about it.*

Journal

Seashell Memories

As she sits alone on her front porch swing,
In view of the beach and rolling sea;
She reflects on seashell memories.

Recalling the times with her sister again,
Two little girls sifting through the white sand;
Telling seashell secrets, as the closest of friends.
Many seashells they found and admired as gold,
Holding them to their lips, after every secret told.
They talked about the future and what it might hold;
Dreaming of marriage and the dress they would wear.
They dreamt their dreams with laughter and care,
Not knowing that life would be so unfair.

Now seashell memories get her through each day,
While she sits and holds each shell, she quietly prays;
And God grants her peace with each passing wave.

John 14:1-4

It is so sad when a loved one or a close friend passes away. Sometimes we feel that we will never see them again. But take heart, we can have hope that we will see them again.

Write down some great memories of a loved one or dear friend, who you have kept close to your heart. Know with faith that you will see each other again someday!

Journal

She Leaves Me Wanting

She leaves me wanting,

Always desiring more.

My love is the ocean,

And hers is the shore.

We embrace every night,

Beneath golden moonlight,

At high tide, we're seen,

Manifesting this dream.

Every morning I long,

To meet with her again.

But the lengths of the days,

Are growing longer my friend.

She leaves me wanting,

Wanting for more.

My love is the ocean,

And hers is the shore.

Song of Solomon 4:9

When we long to be close to someone, we look forward to seeing them with great excitement. We want to spend more and more time with them.

When was the last time that you had the desire to grow in a relationship? Have you ever desired a closer relationship with God? Why or why not?

Journal

The Drawbridge

As I stand beside the troubled waters,
I feel a tugging in the depths of my heart.
I know I must reach the other side,
Yet in comfort, I wish not to part.

I can see a bridge in the distance,
A symbol of hope, calling out my name.
It's the bridge of good foundation,
Offering peace in the place of pain.

It opens up for stranded vessels,
And closes so men can cross,
Above the rushing water,
And the current's wicked toss.

It is Christ the mighty drawbridge,
And God's Spirit is drawing me,
Pulling at my heart and soul,
And helping me to see.

Showing me there's something more,
Awaiting there on the other side,
A place of love and goodness,
Without man's ignorance and pride.

John 3:16

When sin entered the world, we were dead to God. No human could enter into a relationship with Him. God sent His one and only Son, Jesus Christ of Nazareth, so that everyone who believes in him may become children of God. Jesus became the bridge to life when he died for our sins. He did this so that we can come to God, and have everlasting life.

Have you accepted Jesus into your heart? If not, write down a prayer to have him come into your heart. If you have already accepted him, write a short testimony of how it happened and share it with others!

Journal

The Fisherman

An old man sat on a pier.
In one hand he held a fishing pole,
As the other he moved about;
While his stories were being told.

This scene seemed quite silly,
For many times, I did behold;
This fisherman was my father.
I thought him, crazy and old.

He told tales of a young, wise man,
Who once lived by the sea;
A man my father called "Master,"
For a following of fishermen had he.

Some people laughed at him,
And claimed he had lost his mind;
While others would draw near to listen,
At least from time to time.

One day he handed me a Bible,
In brown paper tied with twine.
If only I knew in that moment,
It would be our last goodbye.

Now I'm the old fisherman,
Found sitting on this pier;
With that worn out fishing pole,
I preach to all who will hear.

Sure some people laugh at me,
And claim that I've lost my mind;
But others will draw near to listen,
At least from time to time.

Matthew 4:19

As a Christ follower, Jesus commands us to make disciples of all the nations, meaning that we need to share the good news with others. If we practice what Jesus teaches us, then we will be able to bring others to Christ, just like how a fisherman brings the fish into his boat.

Write down a few Bible verses that you can use to help bring people to Christ, or closer to him.

Journal

The Great Escape

Stranded in the midst of the turquoise sea,

Shipwrecked on the Isle of the Palm Tree;

He scurried down from a canopy of leaves,

From his camouflaged shelter up in the trees.

The day had finally arrived for this castaway.

The island had been his home for many days;

But conditions were right to make his escape,

And down on the beach, his chariot did wait.

He reached the makeshift raft and climbed in,

As the seaward man glanced back at the island;

He noticed the palm trees sway like young maidens,

Waving good-bye to their summertime companions.

2 Corinthians 3:7-11

By trusting the Lord, we are loved, forgiven, and free to live for him. There is freedom in Christ. A celebration of freedom gives us the opportunity to grow closer in our relationship with God.

How have you experienced freedom in your relationship with God, His Son, and His Church?

Journal

The Lonely Starfish

There once was a starfish,
Who laid upon the sand.
On the shores of loneliness,
He washed up on land.
Wondering to himself
Why he'd been so misplaced,
Feeling forgotten by GOD
And taken from his place,
From the abode of the sea,
The depths of Serenity.
It was like heaven to him
Beneath the vessels of men.
As stars enrich heaven,
He had graced the sea floor,
But thereupon land
He was no longer adored.
He laid there silently
Upon that hot and dry sand,
And drifted off to sleep
As if there were no plan…
..Only to awaken
In heaven up above,
To shine amongst his brothers
And emanate God's love!

Psalms 34:17

We sometimes feel that we have been left behind and that no one cares. When we call out to God, He is always there to help us. It may seem at times like He doesn't care, but He cares deeply for His children. He just wants us to depend on Him, and call out to Him.

Write about a time when it felt like you were left behind. Did you turn to the Lord for help?

Journal

The Lord is my Captain

My tattered vessel was in the storm;
My ship was lost at sea.
In the wind, my sail was torn.
The Lord, seeing my boat was worn,
Reached out to rescue me.

Though the storm was mighty strong,
He simply raised his hands up high,
Commanding for the waves to calm,
And the storm winds to subside.

Now the Lord is my captain,
And he fixed the boat just right.
On the journey, much will happen,
But I know those sails are flapping,
So I'll just sit back and enjoy the ride!

Galatians 2:20

In Scripture, the Apostle Paul stated, "I have been crucified with Christ." Let us always remember that Jesus Christ died on the cross for you and for me, and now we are called to put to death our sinful ways and live each day for him, just as Paul did. We are no longer the person we once were.

What are some of the things that have changed in your life, since you or someone you know has become a follower of Christ?

Journal

The Proposal

Two lovers enjoy the sunrise at low tide,
When they witness an exotic surprise;
Wild horses running along the coastline,
Making for a treasurable moment in time.

Both mares and stallions sprinting free,
Like heavenly thoroughbreds,
Straight from a dream.

The young woman watches,
As if in a trance;
Amazed by the stampede,
And the horses' galloping dance.
As they kick up sand,
Along the turquoise sea;
The young man seizes his opportunity.
With gentle hands, he slowly turns her around,
And falls to his knees,
Upon the sand covered ground.

He tells her that he loves her,
And how she is his dream.
He asks her to marry him,
As he pulls out the ring.

Psalms 37:4

To delight in someone means to experience great joy in his or her presence. This can happen once we get to know and understand the person. King David needed to get to know God, so that he could delight in his Creator. It is the same with us today; we must first draw close to the Father through His Son, so that we may delight in Him.

What are some things that you can do to grow closer to God through the body of Christ?

Journal

The Sea of Serenity

I hear it calling out to me,
Through the calmness of my soul;
When my mind is stilled and quiet,
I feel your tender Spirit flow.

I hear the whisper of your waters,
As they move me, by and by,
Like a vessel upon the ocean,
Or the Eagle that takes to fly.

I long to feel the moving wind
That brings these waves, back again,
To move this vessel, through and through,
Bringing me, another glimpse of you.

Your shimmering waters, sustain me,
Beneath the bright and rising Sun.
They're telling me, my journey here,
Has only just begun.

I'm floating as the tender reed,
Always seeking the Spirit that be.
I yearn to sail this uncharted sea,
The sea, they call, Serenity.

All possessions, I have left behind,
In exchange for this wind in my sail.
I explore your waters, hoping to find,
My life, my legacy, a treasurable tale.

But when this journey is complete,
And my body lies down to sleep,
No more sorrow shall I see,
Only the calmness, of Serenity.

Forever, I will drink of your deep,
The waters stir and I am set free.
When this vessel, you no longer see,
Know that I am one with Serenity.

1Peter 1:3-7

To be "born again" means that you are born of God's Spirit. We have a natural birth in the physical world, but when we accept Jesus as our Savior, we are born again of the Spirit. Eternal life begins when we trust Christ and join God's family. According to the Apostle, Peter, our Heavenly Father will help us stay true to our faith even during the difficult times.

How has being "born again" given new meaning to your life?

Journal

The Tugboat

Following a beacon in from the sea,
I noticed a boat hastening out toward me.

When nearing the harbor, it was you, I did see,
Across the restless water, coming out to greet me!

You pulled me forward with increasing pace,
Tugged at my heart, and showed me my place.

You brought me through many hardships and trials,
And helped me along life's final miles.

You carried the weight of my burdens to shore,
And gave me a safe haven in mercy's harbor.

There I did anchor and fastened my ropes.
My vessel was tugged in, by GOD's might boat!

Psalms 18:2

God's protection is limitless. Do you believe this?

There are five characteristics that King David used to describe God: (1) He is a rock, that can't be moved by any who would harm us; (2) He is a fortress or place of safety where the enemy can't follow; (3) He is a shield that comes between us and harm; (4) He is the power that saves us; and, (5) He is a place of safety, high above our enemies. When looking for protection, we must look to our Heavenly Father.

What are five characteristics that you would use to describe God?

Journal

Through Shades of Blue

Through a veil of deep blue,
There's a way, honest and true;
Beyond a constant rain,
A light beyond the pain.

A destination worthwhile,
Though we travel many miles;
Through the world that is lost,
Filled with heartaches and trials.

Still, we continue the journey,
Through shades of blue;
Seeking God's luminous light,
Beyond this ocean of blue.

Psalms 119:105

Have you ever walked into a dimly lit place without a flashlight?

When we bring a flashlight with us, it helps us see those things that can get in our way and make us stumble. When we are in the Bible studying, we are allowing it to be our guide, so that we can stay on the right path.

What Bible verses encourage you when you need help along your journey?

Journal

Visions of Life

As I step out on the waters,

The Lord, He walks beside me;

We speak about the trials,

And all the precious memories.

Glimpses from the life I once knew,

Seem more like passing dreams;

As we walk across the waves,

Like steps in mild terrain.

There are projections overhead,

Stretching across the sky above;

Images of strangers and friends,

And the family whom I love.

In an instant, the sky opens up,

Unveiling the Father's glory;

As the waters all recede,

Revealing His never-ending story.

2 Corinthians 5:8

Facing the unknown may give us anxiety. When we believe in Jesus, we can share the hope and confidence of eternal life with Christ. This world is our temporary home; our real home is in the Kingdom of God.

Write about a time you felt the comfort of the Lord when you experienced the loss of a loved one.

Journal

Wedding on the Beach

Barefoot on the beach they stand,
Two lovers hand in hand;
Looking intently into one another's eyes,
Sharing their vows beneath a blue sky.

Each of them speaking words from the heart,
Making a promise, until death not to part.

A bond of love is being formed this day,
As these two bodies become as one;
On the edge of this seemingly endless sea,
Beneath the rays of a midday sun.

God, family, and friends are witnesses here,
Beholding this beautiful sight;
As these two souls join together in love,
And two hearts begin to unite.

They place their wedding bands,
Upon each other's hands.
It's a beautiful sight to be seen.
Their love is forever represented here,
By these two encircling rings.

They're a reminder of the true circle of love,
Man, his wife, and God above.

Let them never forget this holy bond,
And Heavenly Father, remind them always
To seek your love from beyond.

Now as they move forward from here,
Lord, I pray you will bless all of their plans;
As they leave behind this cherished moment in time,
And their two sets of footprints in the sand.

Genesis 2:24

At a wedding ceremony, two people stand before God, family, and friends proclaiming their true love for each other. It was intended for a man to leave his parents and to commit himself to his wife. The two are joined together as man and wife by taking responsibility for one another's welfare, and loving each other for life.

Is this how you would like your marriage to be? How do you think marriage displays balance and unity within God's creation?

Journal

When My Ship Comes In

As I sit here on this dock,
I wait patiently for when;
The day finally comes,
And my ship comes in.

It's like I've been born again,
Sitting here on this dock;
Like I'm waiting for a long, lost friend,
I skim another rock…

..Across the Sea of Serenity
And toward the other side.
I wait with faith and humility,
And surrender all my pride.

I gaze across this vast ocean,
To the distant and fading horizon,
With faithfulness and such devotion,
To that place, where the sun is rising.

Waiting until her sails appear,
Beneath a noonday sun;
When my ship draws ever near,
And my work is finally done.

Psalms 62:5

Perhaps we have been waiting for something to happen for a long time now, but we feel that we are losing some of our hope. Praying to our Heavenly Father and our Lord Jesus Christ will help us through our times of emotional stress. Christ said he would never leave us; he is right there with us. We just need to talk with God's Spirit and listen to what He has to say. Prayer can release our frustrations and lift our burdens.

What are some of the ways that you pray and seek the Lord's help? Has prayer helped you in the past?

Journal

Conclusion by Tina Bryant

"Whether you have just received Christ in your heart, or you have been a Christ follower for many years, we all go through tough storms in life. Sometimes we may feel a little hopeless, thinking that God doesn't really care or that He is not listening to our prayers. When we trust our Heavenly Father and truly know that He is always there with us, then we are free to live a life of serenity in our Father's sea of grace."

Bonus Poem by Author, Lucy Wilkes

The Little Seashells

The little seashells are gifts from God.
Tiny treasures swell,
As the ocean gives a nod.

Great and small are they,
Where creatures long ago did dwell,
In these houses of a sort,
The little seashells.

Waterfront Romance (Bonus Poem)

Waterfront romance is a getaway for two,

To this charming, southern city;

Where there's always something to do.

You may stroll along the river walk,

Beside the great Cape Fear;

Where you can talk all through the night,

With the one that you hold dear.

You may enjoy a sunset dinner cruise,

With the finest glass of wine;

Or a restaurant on the water's edge,

Might be your choice to dine.

You may ride a horse-drawn carriage,

Along historical, stoned roads;

And stroll through quaint galleries,

Where sweetheart gifts are sold.

Or leave footprints in the sand,

As you walk beneath a pier;

Enjoying carefree romance,

Until the morning sun appears.

~ Chad Joseph Thieman   (Wilmington, NC)

Chad and Tina in

Wilmington, North Carolina

"I lived in Wilmington for three years with my two brothers. It was in this charming city that I received inspiration for many of the poems within this book. I am glad that I am able to watch Tina, as she begins to fall in love with this gem of a city that I so greatly treasure." – *Chad*

About Author, Chad Joseph Thieman:

"I consider writing my spiritual gift, not a natural one by any means. This spiritual gift was given to me in my teen years, immediately after making the commitment to live my life for God the Father, and our Lord Jesus Christ. I first received the desire to inspire others and live with an eternal purpose from the Spirit of Grace, after I moved from Perrysburg, Ohio to the Foothills of the Blue Ridge Mountains in North Carolina (1992). It soon became apparent that I would serve the Lord through writing, which I previously struggled greatly with.

I have believed in God, and have sought a deeper relationship with my Heavenly Father since coming to faith as a young child; but it was the decision to surrender completely, truly repenting of my sin, and choosing to live for Him, that changed my life forever back in those teen years.

I have since been blessed with publishing a three book trilogy series of 101 Treasurable Poems, available at Amazon.com. I am currently working on the *Seasons of Poetry Series, The Way of Wisdom Series,* as well as, a poetry novel entitled *Seashell Memories from Pelican Bay.*"

About Author, Tina Bryant:

"I met Chad and moved to North Carolina in 2015. I was born and raised in Maumee, Ohio. During my adult years, I had been struggling with being single. It wasn't until I turned my life over to Christ, that I truly understood that it was okay to be single. In 2016 I published my first book, *A Quest for Jesus: 31 Day Devotional for Singles,* about my singleness season, and what God had done with me during that time.

God reminded me of Jeremiah 29:11 that I needed to be patient with God. He is never late, He is always on time. *A Quest for Jesus* is a devotional book to help others understand that they are not alone in their singleness.

Chad and I both felt God leading us to write a book together, *Sea of Serenity.* With his spiritual gift in poetry and mine in devotional writing, we both knew this would be a great accomplishment for the Kingdom of God. I really hope you enjoyed it."

If you love the poetry in this book, you may want to check out Chad's previous book: *101 Treasurable Poems of Body, Soul, and Spirit.*

If you love the devotions in this book, you may want to check out Tina's previous book: *A Quest for Jesus: 31 Day Devotional for Singles.*

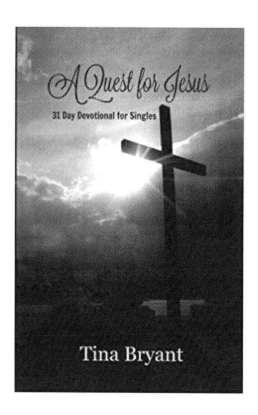

"The Father's Spirit calls to you and to me, as deep calls unto deep; for the believer to come into His presence, and sail the waters of Serenity."

- CJT

Psalms 42:7-8

Made in the USA
Lexington, KY
09 October 2018